FOREWORD

The collection of "Everything Will Be Okay" travel phrasebooks published by T&P Books is designed for people traveling abroad for tourism and business. The phrasebooks contain what matters most - the essentials for basic communication. This is an indispensable set of phrases to "survive" while abroad.

This phrasebook will help you in most cases where you need to ask something, get directions, find out how much something costs, etc. It can also resolve difficult communication situations where gestures just won't help.

This book contains a lot of phrases that have been grouped according to the most relevant topics. You'll also find a mini dictionary with useful words - numbers, time, calendar, colors...

Take "Everything Will Be Okay" phrasebook with you on the road and you'll have an irreplaceable traveling companion who will help you find your way out of any situation and teach you to not fear speaking with foreigners.

TABLE OF CONTENTS

T&P Books Publishing

PRONUNCIATION

T&P phonetic alphabet	Bulgarian example	English example
[a]	сладък [sládək]	shorter than in ask
[e]	череша [ʧeréʃa]	elm, medal
[i]	килим [kilím]	shorter than in feet
[o]	отломка [otlómka]	pod, John
[u]	улуча [ulúʧa]	book
[ə]	въже [vəʒé]	Schwa, rediced 'e'
[ja], [ʲa]	вечеря [veʧérʲa]	royal
[ʲu]	ключ [klʲuʧ]	cued, cute
[ʲo]	фризьор [frizʲór]	New York
[ja], [ʲa] ⁻	история [istórija]	royal
[b]	събота [sébota]	baby, book
[d]	пладне [pládne]	day, doctor
[f]	парфюм [parfʲúm]	face, food
[g]	гараж [garáʒ]	game, gold
[ʒ]	мрежа [mréʒa]	forge, pleasure
[j]	двубой [dvubój]	yes, New York
[h]	храбър [hrábər]	huge, hat
[k]	колело [koleló]	clock, kiss
[l]	паралел [paralél]	lace, people
[m]	мяукам [mʲaúkam]	magic, milk
[n]	фонтан [fontán]	name, normal
[p]	пушек [púʃek]	pencil, private
[r]	крепост [krépost]	rice, radio
[s]	каса [kása]	city, boss
[t]	тютюн [tʲutʲún]	tourist, trip
[v]	завивам [zavívam]	very, river
[ts]	църква [tsérkva]	cats, tsetse fly
[ʃ]	шапка [ʃápka]	machine, shark
[ʧ]	чорапи [ʧorápi]	church, French
[w]	уиски [wíski]	vase, winter
[z]	зарзават [zarzavát]	zebra, please

5

LIST OF ABBREVIATIONS

English abbreviations

ab.	-	about
adj	-	adjective
adv	-	adverb
anim.	-	animate
as adj	-	attributive noun used as adjective
e.g.	-	for example
etc.	-	et cetera
fam.	-	familiar
fem.	-	feminine
form.	-	formal
inanim.	-	inanimate
masc.	-	masculine
math	-	mathematics
mil.	-	military
n	-	noun
pl	-	plural
pron.	-	pronoun
sb	-	somebody
sing.	-	singular
sth	-	something
v aux	-	auxiliary verb
vi	-	intransitive verb
vi, vt	-	intransitive, transitive verb
vt	-	transitive verb

Bulgarian abbreviations

ж	-	feminine noun
ж мн	-	feminine plural
м	-	masculine noun
м мн	-	masculine plural
м, ж	-	masculine, feminine
мн	-	plural
с	-	neuter
с мн	-	neuter plural

BULGARIAN PHRASEBOOK

This section contains important phrases that may come in handy in various real-life situations.
The phrasebook will help you ask for directions, clarify a price, buy tickets, and order food at a restaurant

T&P Books Publishing

PHRASEBOOK
CONTENTS

Travel phrasebooks collection
«Everything Will Be Okay!»

T&P Books Publishing

PHRASEBOOK
- BULGARIAN -

THE MOST IMPORTANT PHRASES

This phrasebook contains
the most important
phrases and questions
for basic communication
Everything you need
to survive overseas

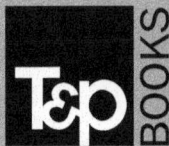

T&P BOOKS

By Andrey Taranov

Phrasebook + 250-word dictionary

English-Bulgarian phrasebook & mini dictionary

By Andrey Taranov

The collection of "Everything Will Be Okay" travel phrasebooks published by T&P Books is designed for people traveling abroad for tourism and business. The phrasebooks contain what matters most - the essentials for basic communication. This is an indispensable set of phrases to "survive" while abroad.

You'll also find a mini dictionary with 250 useful words required for everyday communication - the names of months and days of the week, measurements, family members, and more.

T&P Books Publishing
www.tpbooks.com

ISBN: 978-1-78492-417-1

This book is also available in E-book formats.
Please visit www.tpbooks.com or the major online bookstores.

T&P Books Publishing

The bare minimum

Excuse me, ...	**Извинете, ...** [izvinéte, ...]
Hello.	**Здравейте.** [zdravéjte]
Thank you.	**Благодаря.** [blagodar'á]
Good bye.	**Довиждане.** [dovíʒdane]
Yes.	**Да.** [da]
No.	**Не.** [ne]
I don't know.	**Аз не знам.** [az ne znam]
Where? | Where to? | When?	**Къде? | Накъде? | Кога?** [kədé? | nakədé? | kogá?]
I need ...	**Трябва ми ...** [tr'ábva mi ...]
I want ...	**Аз искам ...** [az ískam ...]
Do you have ...?	**Имате ли ...?** [ímate li ...?]
Is there a ... here?	**Тук има ли ...?** [tuk íma li ...?]
May I ...?	**Мога ли ...?** [móga li ...?]
..., please (polite request)	**Моля.** [mól'a]
I'm looking for ...	**Аз търся ...** [az tərs'a ...]
the restroom	**тоалетна** [toalétna]
an ATM	**банкомат** [bankomát]
a pharmacy (drugstore)	**аптека** [aptéka]
a hospital	**болница** [bólnitsa]
the police station	**полицейски участък** [politséjski uʧástək]
the subway	**метро** [metró]

a taxi	**такси** [táksi]
the train station	**гара** [gára]

My name is ...	**Казвам се ...** [kázvam se ...]
What's your name?	**Как се казвате?** [kak se kázvate?]
Could you please help me?	**Помогнете ми, моля.** [pomognéte mi, mólʲa]
I've got a problem.	**Аз имам проблем.** [az ímam problém]
I don't feel well.	**Лошо ми е.** [lóʃo mi e]
Call an ambulance!	**Повикайте бърза помощ!** [povikájte bérza pómoʃt!]
May I make a call?	**Може ли да се обадя?** [móʒe li da se obádʲa?]

I'm sorry.	**Извинявам се.** [izvinʲávam se]
You're welcome.	**Моля.** [mólʲa]

I, me	**аз** [az]
you (inform.)	**ти** [ti]
he	**той** [toj]
she	**тя** [tʲa]
they (masc.)	**те** [te]
they (fem.)	**те** [te]
we	**ние** [nie]
you (pl)	**вие** [víe]
you (sg, form.)	**Вие** [víe]

ENTRANCE	**ВХОД** [vhod]
EXIT	**ИЗХОД** [íshot]
OUT OF ORDER	**НЕ РАБОТИ** [ne ráboti]
CLOSED	**ЗАТВОРЕНО** [zatvóreno]

OPEN	**ОТВОРЕНО** [otvóreno]
FOR WOMEN	**ЗА ЖЕНИ** [za ʒení]
FOR MEN	**ЗА МЪЖЕ** [za məʒé]

Questions

Where?	**Къде?** [kədé?]
Where to?	**Накъде?** [nakədé?]
Where from?	**Откъде?** [otkədé?]
Why?	**Защо?** [zaʃtó?]
For what reason?	**По каква причина?** [po kakvá pritʃína?]
When?	**Кога?** [kogá?]
How long?	**За колко?** [za kólko?]
At what time?	**В колко?** [v kólko?]
How much?	**Колко струва?** [kólko strúva?]
Do you have ...?	**Имате ли ...?** [ímate li ...?]
Where is ...?	**Къде се намира ...?** [kədé se namíra ...?]
What time is it?	**Колко е часът?** [kólko e ʧasét?]
May I make a call?	**Може ли да се обадя?** [moʒe li da se obádʲa?]
Who's there?	**Кой е там?** [koj e tam?]
Can I smoke here?	**Мога ли тук да пуша?** [móga li tuk da púʃa?]
May I ...?	**Мога ли ...?** [móga li ...?]

Needs

I'd like …	Аз бих искал /искала/ … [az bih ískal /ískala/ …]
I don't want …	Аз не искам … [az ne ískam …]
I'm thirsty.	Аз искам да пия. [az ískam da pijá]
I want to sleep.	Аз искам да спя. [az ískam da spʲa]

I want …	Аз искам … [az ískam …]
to wash up	да се измия [da se izmijá]
to brush my teeth	да си мия зъбите [da si míja zəbíte]
to rest a while	малко да си почина [málko da si potʃína]
to change my clothes	да се преоблека [da se preobleká]

to go back to the hotel	да се върна в хотела [da se vérna v hotéla]
to buy …	да купя … [da kúpʲa …]
to go to …	да отида … [da otída …]
to visit …	да посетя … [da posetʲá …]
to meet with …	да се срещна с … [da se sréʃtna s …]
to make a call	да се обадя [da se obádʲa]

I'm tired.	Аз се изморих. [az se izmoríh]
We are tired.	Ние се изморихме. [nie se izmoríhme]
I'm cold.	Студено ми е. [studéno mi e]
I'm hot.	Топло ми е. [tóplo mi e]
I'm OK.	Нормално ми е. [normálno mi e]

I need to make a call.	**Трябва да се обадя.** [triábva da se obádja]
I need to go to the restroom.	**Искам да отида в тоалетната.** [ískam da otída v toalétnata]
I have to go.	**Трябва да тръгвам.** [triábva da trégvam]
I have to go now.	**Сега трябва да тръгвам.** [segá triábva da trégvam]

Asking for directions

Excuse me, ...	Извинете, ... [izvinéte, ...]
Where is ...?	Къде се намира ...? [kədé se namíra ...?]
Which way is ...?	В коя посока се намира ...? [v koja posóka se namíra ...?]
Could you help me, please?	Помогнете ми, моля. [pomognéte mi, mólʲa]

I'm looking for ...	Аз търся ... [az térsʲa ...]
I'm looking for the exit.	Аз търся изход. [az térsʲa íshot]
I'm going to ...	Аз пътувам до ... [az pətúvam do ...]
Am I going the right way to ...?	Правилно ли вървя ...? [právilno li vərvʲá ...?]

Is it far?	Далече ли е? [dalétʃe li e?]
Can I get there on foot?	Ще стигна ли дотам пеша? [ʃte stígna li dotám péʃa?]
Can you show me on the map?	Покажете ми на картата, моля. [pokaʒéte mi na kártata, mólʲa]
Show me where we are right now.	Покажете, къде сме сега. [pokaʒéte, kədé sme segá]

Here	Тук [tuk]
There	Там [tam]
This way	Тука [túka]

Turn right.	Завийте надясно. [zavíjte nadʲásno]
Turn left.	Завийте наляво. [zavíjte nalʲávo]
first (second, third) turn	първи (втори, трети) завой [pərvi (ftóri, tréti) zavój]
to the right	надясно [nadʲásno]

to the left

наляво
[nalʲávo]

Go straight ahead.

Вървете направо.
[vərvéte naprávo]

Signs

WELCOME!	**ДОБРЕ ДОШЛИ!** [dobré doʃlí!]
ENTRANCE	**ВХОД** [vhod]
EXIT	**ИЗХОД** [íshot]
PUSH	**БУТНИ** [butní]
PULL	**ДРЪПНИ** [drəpní]
OPEN	**ОТВОРЕНО** [otvóreno]
CLOSED	**ЗАТВОРЕНО** [zatvóreno]
FOR WOMEN	**ЗА ЖЕНИ** [za ʒení]
FOR MEN	**ЗА МЪЖЕ** [za məʒé]
GENTLEMEN, GENTS	**МЪЖКА ТОАЛЕТНА** [méʒka toalétna]
WOMEN	**ЖЕНСКА ТОАЛЕТНА** [ʒénska toalétna]
DISCOUNTS	**НАМАЛЕНИЯ** [namalénija]
SALE	**РАЗПРОДАЖБА** [rasprodáʒba]
FREE	**БЕЗПЛАТНО** [besplátno]
NEW!	**НОВИНА!** [noviná!]
ATTENTION!	**ВНИМАНИЕ!** [vnimánie!]
NO VACANCIES	**НЯМА МЕСТА** [nʲáma mestá]
RESERVED	**РЕЗЕРВИРАНО** [rezervírano]
ADMINISTRATION	**АДМИНИСТРАЦИЯ** [administrátsija]
STAFF ONLY	**САМО ЗА ПЕРСОНАЛА** [sámo za personála]

BEWARE OF THE DOG!	**ЛОШО КУЧЕ** [lóʃo kutʃe]
NO SMOKING!	**НЕ СЕ ПУШИ!** [ne se púʃi!]
DO NOT TOUCH!	**НЕ ПИПАЙ С РЪЦЕТЕ!** [ne pipáj s rətséte!]
DANGEROUS	**ОПАСНО** [opásno]
DANGER	**ОПАСНОСТ** [opásnost]
HIGH VOLTAGE	**ВИСОКО НАПРЕЖЕНИЕ** [visóko napreʒénie]
NO SWIMMING!	**КЪПАНЕТО Е ЗАБРАНЕНО** [kəpaneto e zabranéno]
OUT OF ORDER	**НЕ РАБОТИ** [ne ráboti]
FLAMMABLE	**ОГНЕОПАСНО** [ogneopásno]
FORBIDDEN	**ЗАБРАНЕНО** [zabranéno]
NO TRESPASSING!	**ПРЕМИНАВАНЕТО Е ЗАБРАНЕНО** [preminávaneto e zabranéno]
WET PAINT	**БОЯДИСАНО** [bojadísano]
CLOSED FOR RENOVATIONS	**ЗАТВОРЕНО ЗА РЕМОНТ** [zatvóreno za remónt]
WORKS AHEAD	**РЕМОНТНИ РАБОТИ** [remóntni ráboti]
DETOUR	**ЗАОБИКАЛЯНЕ** [zaobikálʲane]

Transportation. General phrases

plane	**самолет** [samolét]
train	**влак** [vlak]
bus	**автобус** [aftobús]
ferry	**фериот** [féribot]
taxi	**такси** [táksi]
car	**кола** [kóla]

schedule	**разписание** [raspisánie]
Where can I see the schedule?	**Къде мога да видя разписанието?** [kədé móga da vídʲa raspisánieto?]
workdays (weekdays)	**работни дни** [rabótni dni]
weekends	**почивни дни** [potʃívni dni]
holidays	**празнични дни** [práznitʃni dni]

DEPARTURE	**ЗАМИНАВАНЕ** [zaminávane]
ARRIVAL	**ПРИСТИГАНЕ** [pristígane]
DELAYED	**ЗАКЪСНЯВА** [zakəsnʲáva]
CANCELLED	**ОТМЕНЕН** [otmenén]

next (train, etc.)	**следващ** [slédvaʃt]
first	**първи** [pərvi]
last	**последен** [posléden]

When is the next ...?	**Кога е следващият ...?** [kogá e slédvaʃtijat ...?]
When is the first ...?	**Кога тръгва първият ...?** [kogá trégva pérvijat ...?]

When is the last ...?   **Кога тръгва последният ...?**
[kogá trégva póslednijat ...?]

transfer (change of trains, etc.)   **прекачване**
[prekátʃvane]

to make a transfer   **да правя прекачване**
[da právʲa prekátʃvane]

Do I need to make a transfer?   **Трябва ли да правя прекачване?**
[trʲábva li da právʲa prekátʃvane?]

Buying tickets

Where can I buy tickets?	**Къде мога да купя билети?** [kədé móga da kúpʲa biléti?]
ticket	**билет** [bilét]
to buy a ticket	**да купя билет** [da kúpʲa bilét]
ticket price	**цена на билета** [tsená na biléta]

Where to?	**Накъде?** [nakədé?]
To what station?	**До коя станция?** [do kojá stántsija?]
I need ...	**Трябва ми ...** [trʲábva mi ...]
one ticket	**един билет** [edín bilét]
two tickets	**два билета** [dva biléta]
three tickets	**три билета** [tri biléta]

one-way	**в една посока** [v edná posóka]
round-trip	**отиване и връщане** [otívane i vréʃtane]
first class	**първа класа** [pérva klása]
second class	**втора класа** [ftóra klása]

today	**днес** [dnes]
tomorrow	**утре** [útre]
the day after tomorrow	**вдругиден** [vdrúgiden]
in the morning	**сутринта** [sutrínta]
in the afternoon	**през деня** [prez denʲá]
in the evening	**вечерта** [vetʃertá]

aisle seat

място до коридора
[mʲásto do koridóra]

window seat

място до прозореца
[mʲásto do prozóretsa]

How much?

Колко?
[kólko?]

Can I pay by credit card?

Мога ли да платя с карта?
[móga li da platʲá s kárta?]

Bus

bus	**автобус** [aftobús]
intercity bus	**междуградски автобус** [meʒdugrátski aftobús]
bus stop	**автобусна спирка** [aftobúsna spírka]
Where's the nearest bus stop?	**Къде се намира най-близката автобусна спирка?** [kədé se namíra naj-blízkata aftobúsna spírka?]

number (bus ~, etc.)	**номер** [nómer]
Which bus do I take to get to …?	**Кой номер автобус отива до …?** [koj nómer aftobús otíva do …?]
Does this bus go to …?	**Този автобус отива ли до …?** [tózi aftobús otíva li do …?]
How frequent are the buses?	**Кога има автобуси?** [kogá íma aftobúsi?]

every 15 minutes	**на всеки 15 минути** [na fséki petnádeset minúti]
every half hour	**на всеки половин час** [na fséki polovín ʧas]
every hour	**на всеки час** [na fséki ʧas]
several times a day	**няколко пъти на ден** [nʲákolko péti na den]
… times a day	**… пъти на ден** [… péti na den]

schedule	**разписание** [raspisánie]
Where can I see the schedule?	**Къде мога да видя разписанието?** [kədé móga da vídʲa raspisánieto?]
When is the next bus?	**Кога е следващият автобус?** [kogá e slédvaʃtijat aftobús?]
When is the first bus?	**Кога тръгва първият автобус?** [kogá trəgva pérvijat aftobús?]
When is the last bus?	**Кога заминава последният автобус?** [kogá zamináva poslédnijat aftobús?]

stop

спирка
[spírka]

next stop

следваща спирка
[slédvaʃta spírka]

last stop (terminus)

последна спирка
[poslédna spírka]

Stop here, please.

Спрете тук, моля.
[spréte tuk, mólʲa]

Excuse me, this is my stop.

Може ли, това е моята спирка.
[móʒe li, tová e mójata spírka]

Train

train	**влак** [vlak]
suburban train	**крайградски влак** [krajgrátski vlak]
long-distance train	**влак за далечни разстояния** [vlak za dalétʃni rasstojánija]
train station	**гара** [gára]
Excuse me, where is the exit to the platform?	**Извинявайте, къде е изхода** **към влаковете?** [izvinʲávajte, kədé e íshoda kəm vlákovete?]

Does this train go to …?	**Този влак отива ли до …?** [tózi vlak otíva li do …?]
next train	**следващ влак** [slédvaʃt vlak]
When is the next train?	**Кога е следващият влак?** [kogá e slédvaʃtijat vlak?]
Where can I see the schedule?	**Къде мога да видя разписанието?** [kədé móga da vídʲa raspisánieto?]
From which platform?	**От кой перон?** [ot koj perón?]
When does the train arrive in …?	**Кога влакът пристига в …?** [kogá vlákət pristíga v …?]

Please help me.	**Помогнете ми, моля.** [pomognéte mi, mólʲa]
I'm looking for my seat.	**Аз търся мястото си.** [az térsʲa mʲástoto si]
We're looking for our seats.	**Ние търсим местата си.** [nie térsim mestáta si]

My seat is taken.	**Мястото ми е заето.** [mʲástoto mi e zaéto]
Our seats are taken.	**Местата ни са заети.** [mestáta ni sa zaéti]
I'm sorry but this is my seat.	**Извинявайте, но това е** **моето място.** [izvinʲávajte, no tová e móeto mʲásto]

Is this seat taken?   **Това място свободно ли е?**
[tová m^jásto svobódno li e?]

May I sit here?   **Мога ли да седна тук?**
[móga li da sédna tuk?]

On the train. Dialogue (No ticket)

Ticket, please.
Билета ви, моля.
[biléta vi, mólʲa]

I don't have a ticket.
Аз нямам билет.
[az nʲámam bilét]

I lost my ticket.
Аз загубих билета си.
[az zagúbih biléta si]

I forgot my ticket at home.
Аз забравих билета си в къщи.
[az zabrávih biléta si v kéʃti]

You can buy a ticket from me.
Вие можете да си купите билет от мен.
[víe móʒete da si kúpite bilét ot men]

You will also have to pay a fine.
Също така ще трябва да заплатите глоба.
[séʃto taká ʃte trʲábva da zaplátite glóba]

Okay.
Добре.
[dobré]

Where are you going?
Накъде пътувате?
[nakədé pətúvate?]

I'm going to ...
Аз пътувам до ...
[az pətúvam do ...]

How much? I don't understand.
Колко? Не разбирам.
[kólko? ne razbíram]

Write it down, please.
Напишете, моля.
[napiʃéte, mólʲa]

Okay. Can I pay with a credit card?
Добре. Мога ли да платя с карта?
[dobré. móga li da platʲá s kárta?]

Yes, you can.
Да. Можете.
[da. móʒete]

Here's your receipt.
Заповядайте, вашата квитанция.
[zapovʲádajte, vaʃata kvitántsija]

Sorry about the fine.
Съжалявам за глобата.
[səʒalʲávam za glóbata]

That's okay. It was my fault.
Няма нищо. Вината е моя.
[nʲáma níʃto. vináta e mója]

Enjoy your trip.
Приятно пътуване.
[prijátno pətúvane]

Taxi

taxi	**такси** [táksi]
taxi driver	**таксист** [táksist]
to catch a taxi	**да взема такси** [da vzéma táksi]
taxi stand	**стоянка на такси** [stojánka na táksi]
Where can I get a taxi?	**Къде мога да взема такси?** [kədé móga da vzéma táksi?]
to call a taxi	**да повикам такси** [da povíkam táksi]
I need a taxi.	**Трябва ми такси.** [trʲábva mi táksi]
Right now.	**Точно сега.** [tótʃno segá]
What is your address (location)?	**Вашият адрес?** [váʃijat adrés?]
My address is ...	**Моят адрес е ...** [mójat adrés e ...]
Your destination?	**Къде отивате?** [kədé otívate?]
Excuse me, ...	**Извинете, ...** [izvinéte, ...]
Are you available?	**Свободни ли сте?** [svobódni li ste?]
How much is it to get to ...?	**Каква е цената до ...?** [kakvá e tsenáta do ...?]
Do you know where it is?	**Знаете ли, къде е това?** [znáete li, kədé e tová?]
Airport, please.	**До аерогарата, моля.** [do aerogárata, mólʲa]
Stop here, please.	**Спрете тук, моля.** [spréte tuk, mólʲa]
It's not here.	**Това не е тук.** [tová ne e tuk]
This is the wrong address.	**Това е неправилен адрес.** [tová e neprávilen adrés]
Turn left.	**наляво** [nalʲávo]
Turn right.	**надясно** [nadʲásno]

How much do I owe you?
Колко ви дължа?
[kólko vi dəlʒá?]

I'd like a receipt, please.
Дайте ми касов бон, моля.
[dájte mi kásov bon, mólʲa]

Keep the change.
Задръжте рестото.
[zadréʒte réstoto]

Would you please wait for me?
Изчакайте ме, моля.
[iztʃákajte me, mólʲa]

five minutes
пет минути
[pet minúti]

ten minutes
десет минути
[déset minúti]

fifteen minutes
петнадесет минути
[petnádeset minúti]

twenty minutes
двадесет минути
[dvádeset minúti]

half an hour
половин час
[polóvin tʃas]

Hotel

Hello.	**Здравейте.** [zdravéjte]
My name is ...	**Казвам се ...** [kázvam se ...]
I have a reservation.	**Аз резервирах стая.** [az rezervírah stája]
I need ...	**Трябва ми ...** [triábva mi ...]
a single room	**единична стая** [edinítʃna stája]
a double room	**двойна стая** [dvójna stája]
How much is that?	**Колко струва?** [kólko strúva?]
That's a bit expensive.	**Това е малко скъпо.** [tová e málko sképo]
Do you have anything else?	**Имате ли още нещо?** [ímate li óʃte néʃto?]
I'll take it.	**Ще го взема.** [ʃte go vzéma]
I'll pay in cash.	**Ще платя в брой.** [ʃte plátʲa v broj]
I've got a problem.	**Аз имам проблем.** [az ímam problém]
My ... is broken.	**Моят /моята/ ... е счупен /счупена/.** [mójat /mójata/ ... e stʃúpen /stʃúpena/]
My ... is out of order.	**Моят /моята/ ... не работи** [mójat /mójata/ ... ne ráboti]
TV	**моят телевизор** [mójat televízor]
air conditioner	**моят климатик** [mójat klímatik]
tap	**моят кран** [mójat kran]
shower	**моят душ** [mójat duʃ]
sink	**моята мивка** [mójata mífka]
safe	**моят сейф** [mójat sejf]

door lock	**моята ключалка** [mójata klʲutʃálka]
electrical outlet	**моят контакт** [mójat kontákt]
hairdryer	**моят сешоар** [mójat seʃoár]

I don't have …	**Нямам …** [nʲámam …]
water	**вода** [vodá]
light	**ток** [tok]
electricity	**електричество** [elektrítʃestvo]

Can you give me …?	**Може ли да ми дадете …?** [móʒe li da mi dadéte …?]
a towel	**хавлия** [havlíja]
a blanket	**одеяло** [odejálo]
slippers	**чехли** [tʃéhli]
a robe	**халат** [halát]
shampoo	**шампоан** [ʃampoán]
soap	**сапун** [sapún]

I'd like to change rooms.	**Бих искал /искала/ да сменя стаята си.** [bih ískal /ískala/ da smenʲá stájata si]
I can't find my key.	**Не мога да намеря ключа си.** [ne móga da namérʲa klʲútʃa si]
Could you open my room, please?	**Отворете моята стая, моля.** [otvórete mójata stája, mólʲa]
Who's there?	**Кой е?** [koj e?]
Come in!	**Влезте!** [vlézte!]
Just a minute!	**Една минута!** [edná minúta!]

Not right now, please.	**Моля, не сега.** [mólʲa, ne segá]
Come to my room, please.	**Влезте при мен, моля.** [vlézte pri men, mólʲa]

I'd like to order food service.

Бих искал /искала/ да поръчам храна за стаята.
[bih ískal /ískala/ da pórətʃam hraná za stájata]

My room number is …

Номерът на стаята ми е ….
[nómerət na stájata mi e ….]

I'm leaving …

Заминавам …
[zaminávam …]

We're leaving …

Ние заминаваме …
[nie zaminávame …]

right now

сега
[segá]

this afternoon

днес след обяд
[dnes slet obʲát]

tonight

днес вечерта
[dnes vetʃertá]

tomorrow

утре
[útre]

tomorrow morning

утре сутринта
[útre sutrínta]

tomorrow evening

утре вечер
[útre vétʃer]

the day after tomorrow

вдругиден
[vdrúgiden]

I'd like to pay.

Бих искал /искала/ да заплатя.
[bih ískal /ískala/ da zaplatʲá]

Everything was wonderful.

Всичко беше отлично.
[fsítʃko béʃe otlítʃno]

Where can I get a taxi?

Къде мога да взема такси?
[kədé móga da vzéma táksi?]

Would you call a taxi for me, please?

Повикайте ми такси, моля.
[povikájte mi táksi, mólʲa]

Restaurant

Can I look at the menu, please?	**Мога ли да видя менюто ви?** [móga li da vídʲa menʲúto vi?]
Table for one.	**Маса за един човек.** [mása za edín tʃovék]
There are two (three, four) of us.	**Ние сме двама (трима, четирима).** [nie sme dváma (tríma, tʃetírima)]

Smoking	**За пушачи** [za puʃátʃi]
No smoking	**За непушачи** [za nepuʃátʃi]
Excuse me! (addressing a waiter)	**Ако обичате!** [ako obitʃate!]
menu	**меню** [menʲú]
wine list	**Карта на виното** [kárta na vínoto]
The menu, please.	**Менюто, моля.** [menʲúto, mólʲa]

Are you ready to order?	**Готови ли сте да поръчате?** [gotóvi li ste da porétʃate?]
What will you have?	**Какво ще поръчате?** [kakvó ʃte porétʃate?]
I'll have ...	**Аз искам ....** [az ískam ....]

I'm a vegetarian.	**Аз съм вегетарианец /вегетарианка/.** [az səm vegetariánets /vegetariánka/]
meat	**месо** [mesó]
fish	**риба** [ríba]
vegetables	**зеленчуци** [zelentʃútsi]
Do you have vegetarian dishes?	**Имате ли вегетариански ястия?** [ímate li vegetariánski jástija?]
I don't eat pork.	**Аз не ям свинско.** [az ne jam svínsko]
Band-Aid	**Той /тя/ не яде месо.** [toj /tʲa/ ne jadé mesó]
I am allergic to ...	**Имам алергия към ...** [ímam alérgija kəm ...]

Would you please bring me ...

Донесете ми, моля ...
[doneséte mi, mólʲa ...]

salt | pepper | sugar

сол | пипер | захар
[sol | pipér | záhar]

coffee | tea | dessert

кафе | чай | десерт
[kafé | tʃaj | desért]

water | sparkling | plain

вода | газирана | негазирана
[vodá | gazírana | negazírana]

a spoon | fork | knife

лъжица | вилица | нож
[ləʒítsa | vílitsa | noʒ]

a plate | napkin

чиния | салфетка
[tʃiníja | salfétka]

Enjoy your meal!

Приятен апетит!
[prijáten apetít!]

One more, please.

Донесете още, моля.
[doneséte óʃte, mólʲa]

It was very delicious.

Беше много вкусно.
[béʃe mnógo fkúsno]

---

check | change | tip

сметка | ресто | бакшиш
[smétka | résto | bakʃíʃ]

Check, please.
(Could I have the check, please?)

Сметката, моля.
[smétkata, mólʲa]

Can I pay by credit card?

Мога ли да платя с карта?
[móga li da platʲá s kárta?]

I'm sorry, there's a mistake here.

Извинявайте, тук има грешка.
[izvinʲávajte, tuk íma gréʃka]

Shopping

Can I help you?
Мога ли да ви помогна?
[móga li da vi pomógna?]

Do you have ...?
Имате ли ...?
[ímate li ...?]

I'm looking for ...
Аз търся ...
[az tŕsʲa ...]

I need ...
Трябва ми ...
[trʲábva mi ...]

I'm just looking.
Само гледам.
[sámo glédam]

We're just looking.
Ние само гледаме.
[nie sámo glédame]

I'll come back later.
Ще дойда по-късно.
[ʃte dójda po-késno]

We'll come back later.
Ние ще дойдем по-късно.
[nie ʃte dójdem po-késno]

discounts | sale
намаления | разпродажба
[namalénija | rasprodáʒba]

Would you please show me ...
Покажете ми, моля ...
[pokaʒéte mi, mólʲa ...]

Would you please give me ...
Дайте ми, моля ...
[dájte mi, mólʲa ...]

Can I try it on?
Може ли да пробвам това?
[móʒe li da próbvam tová?]

Excuse me, where's the fitting room?
Извинявайте, къде може да пробвам това?
[izvinʲávajte, kədé móʒe da próbvam tová?]

Which color would you like?
Какъв цвят желаете?
[kakév tsvʲat ʒeláete?]

size | length
размер | ръст
[razmér | rəst]

How does it fit?
Стана ли ви?
[stána li vi?]

How much is it?
Колко струва това?
[kólko strúva tová?]

That's too expensive.
Това е много скъпо.
[tová e mnógo sképo]

I'll take it.
Ще взема това.
[ʃte vzéma tová]

Excuse me, where do I pay?

Извинявайте, къде е касата?
[izvin'ávajte, kədé e kásata?]

Will you pay in cash or credit card?

Как ще плащате?
В брой или с карта?
[kak ʃte pláʃtate?
v broj íli s kárta?]

In cash | with credit card

в брой | с карта
[v broj | s kárta]

Do you want the receipt?

Трябва ли ви касов бон?
[tr'ábva li vi kásov bon?]

Yes, please.

Да, бъдете така добър.
[da, bədéte taká dobér]

No, it's OK.

Не, не трябва. Благодаря.
[ne, ne tr'ábva. blagodar'á]

Thank you. Have a nice day!

Благодаря. Всичко хубаво!
[blagodar'á. fsítʃko húbavo!]

In town

Excuse me, …	**Извинете, моля …** [izvinéte, mólʲa …]
I'm looking for …	**Аз търся …** [az térsʲa …]
the subway	**метрото** [metróto]
my hotel	**хотела си** [hotéla si]
the movie theater	**киното** [kínoto]
a taxi stand	**стоянката на такси** [stojánkata na táksi]

an ATM	**банкомат** [bankomát]
a foreign exchange office	**обмяна на валута** [obmʲána na valúta]
an internet café	**интернет-кафе** [internét-kafé]
… street	**улица …** [úlitsa …]
this place	**ето това място** [eto tová mʲásto]

Do you know where … is?	**Знаете ли, къде се намира …?** [znáete li, kədé se namíra …?]
Which street is this?	**Как се нарича тази улица?** [kak se narítʃa tázi úlitsa?]
Show me where we are right now.	**Покажете, къде сме сега.** [pokaʒéte, kədé sme segá]
Can I get there on foot?	**Ще стигна ли дотам пеша?** [ʃte stígna li dotám péʃa?]
Do you have a map of the city?	**Имате ли карта на града?** [ímate li kárta na gradá?]

How much is a ticket to get in?	**Колко струва билет за вход?** [kólko strúva bilét za vhot?]
Can I take pictures here?	**Тук може ли да се снима?** [tuk móʒe li da se snimá?]
Are you open?	**Отворено ли е?** [otvóreno li e?]

When do you open? **В колко отваряте?**
[v kólko otvárʲate?]

When do you close? **До колко часа работите?**
[do kólko ʧása rábotite?]

Money

money	**пари** [parí]
cash	**пари в брой** [parí v broj]
paper money	**книжни пари** [kníʒni parí]
loose change	**дребни пари** [drébni parí]
check | change | tip	**сметка | ресто | бакшиш** [smétka | résto | bakʃíʃ]

credit card	**кредитна карта** [kréditna kárta]
wallet	**портмоне** [portmoné]
to buy	**да купя** [da kúpʲa]
to pay	**да платя** [da platʲá]
fine	**глоба** [glóba]
free	**безплатно** [besplátno]

Where can I buy ...?	**Къде мога да купя ...?** [kədé móga da kúpʲa ...?]
Is the bank open now?	**Отворена ли е банката сега ?** [otvórena li e bánkata segá ?]
When does it open?	**В колко се отваря?** [v kólko se otvárʲa?]
When does it close?	**До колко часа работи?** [do kólko tʃása ráboti?]

How much?	**Колко?** [kólko?]
How much is this?	**Колко струва?** [kólko strúva?]
That's too expensive.	**Това е много скъпо.** [tová e mnógo sképo]

Excuse me, where do I pay?	**Извинявайте, къде е касата?** [izvinʲávajte, kədé e kásata?]
Check, please.	**Сметката, моля.** [smétkata, mólʲa]

Can I pay by credit card? | **Мога ли да платя с карта?**
[móga li da platⁱá s kárta?]

Is there an ATM here? | **Тук има ли банкомат?**
[tuk íma li bankomát?]

I'm looking for an ATM. | **Трябва ми банкомат.**
[trⁱábva mi bankomát]

I'm looking for a foreign exchange office. | **Аз търся обмяна на валута.**
[az térsⁱa obmⁱána na valúta]

I'd like to change … | **Бих искал да сменя …**
[bih ískal da smenⁱá …]

What is the exchange rate? | **Какъв е курсът?**
[kakév e kúrsət?]

Do you need my passport? | **Трябва ли ви паспортът ми?**
[trⁱábva li vi paspórtət mi?]

Time

What time is it?	**Колко е часът?** [kólko e ʧasét?]
When?	**Кога?** [kogá?]
At what time?	**В колко?** [v kólko?]
now	later	after …	**сега	по-късно	след …** [segá	po-késno	slet …]

one o'clock	**един часа** [edín ʧása]
one fifteen	**един часа и петнадесет минути** [edín ʧása i petnádeset minúti]
one thirty	**един часа и тридесет минути** [edín ʧása i trídeset minúti]
one forty-five	**два без петнадесет** [dva bez petnádeset]

one	two	three	**един	два	три** [edín	dva	tri]
four	five	six	**четири	пет	шест** [ʧétiri	pet	ʃest]
seven	eight	nine	**седем	осем	девет** [sédem	ósem	dévet]
ten	eleven	twelve	**десет	единадесет	дванадесет** [déset	edinádeset	dvanádeset]

in …	**след …** [slet …]
five minutes	**пет минути** [pet minúti]
ten minutes	**десет минути** [déset minúti]
fifteen minutes	**петнадесет минути** [petnádeset minúti]
twenty minutes	**двадесет минути** [dvádeset minúti]
half an hour	**половин час** [polóvin ʧas]
an hour	**един час** [edín ʧas]

in the morning	сутринта
	[sutrínta]
early in the morning	рано сутринта
	[ráno sutrínta]
this morning	днес сутринта
	[dnes sutrínta]
tomorrow morning	утре сутринта
	[útre sutrínta]

in the middle of the day	на обяд
	[na obʲád]
in the afternoon	след обяд
	[slet obʲát]
in the evening	вечерта
	[vetʃertá]
tonight	днес вечерта
	[dnes vetʃertá]

at night	през нощта
	[prez noʃtá]
yesterday	вчера
	[vtʃéra]
today	днес
	[dnes]
tomorrow	утре
	[útre]
the day after tomorrow	вдругиден
	[vdrúgiden]

What day is it today?	Какъв ден е днес?
	[kakév den e dnes?]
It's ...	Днес е ...
	[dnes e ...]
Monday	понеделник
	[ponedélnik]
Tuesday	вторник
	[ftórnik]
Wednesday	сряда
	[srʲáda]

Thursday	четвъртък
	[tʃetvértək]
Friday	петък
	[pétək]
Saturday	събота
	[sébota]
Sunday	неделя
	[nedélʲa]

Greetings. Introductions

Hello.	**Здравейте.** [zdravéjte]
Pleased to meet you.	**Радвам се, че се запознахме.** [rádvam se, ʧe se zapoznáhme]
Me too.	**И аз.** [i az]
I'd like you to meet ...	**Запознайте се. Това е ...** [zapoznájte se. tová e ...]
Nice to meet you.	**Много ми е приятно.** [mnógo mi e prijátno]

How are you?	**Как сте?** [kak ste?]
My name is ...	**Казвам се ...** [kázvam se ...]
His name is ...	**Той се казва ...** [toj se kázva ...]
Her name is ...	**Тя се казва ...** [tʲa se kázva ...]
What's your name?	**Как се казвате?** [kak se kázvate?]
What's his name?	**Как се казва той?** [kak se kázva toj?]
What's her name?	**Как се казва тя?** [kak se kázva tʲa?]

What's your last name?	**Как ви е фамилията?** [kak vi e famílijata?]
You can call me ...	**Наричайте ме ...** [narítʃajte me ...]
Where are you from?	**Откъде сте?** [otkədé ste?]
I'm from ...	**Аз съм от ...** [az səm ot ...]
What do you do for a living?	**Като какъв работите?** [kató kakév rábotite?]
Who is this?	**Кой сте?** [koj ste?]
Who is he?	**Кой е той?** [koj e toj?]
Who is she?	**Коя е тя?** [kojá e tʲa?]
Who are they?	**Кои са те?** [koi sa te?]

This is …	**Това е …** [tová e …]
my friend (masc.)	**моят приятел** [mójat prijátel]
my friend (fem.)	**моята приятелка** [mójata prijátelka]
my husband	**моят мъж** [mójat məʒ]
my wife	**моята жена** [mójata ʒená]
my father	**моят баща** [mójat baʃtá]
my mother	**моята майка** [mójata májka]
my brother	**моят брат** [mójat brat]
my sister	**моята сестра** [mójata sestrá]
my son	**моят син** [mójat sin]
my daughter	**моята дъщеря** [mójata dəʃterʲá]
This is our son.	**Това е нашият син.** [tová e náʃijat sin]
This is our daughter.	**Това е нашата дъщеря.** [tová e náʃata dəʃterʲá]
These are my children.	**Това са моите деца.** [tová sa móite detsá]
These are our children.	**Това са нашите деца.** [tová sa náʃite detsá]

Farewells

Good bye!
Довиждане!
[dovíʒdane!]

Bye! (inform.)
Чао!
[tʃao!]

See you tomorrow.
До утре!
[do útre!]

See you soon.
До срещата!
[do sréʃtata!]

See you at seven.
Ще се срещнем в седем.
[ʃte se sréʃtnem v sédem]

Have fun!
Забавлявайте се!
[zabavlʲávajte se!]

Talk to you later.
Ще поговорим по-късно.
[ʃte pogovórim po-kásno]

Have a nice weekend.
Успешен уикенд!
[uspéʃen uíkend!]

Good night.
Лека нощ.
[léka noʃt]

It's time for me to go.
Сега трябва да тръгвам.
[segá trʲábva da trégvam]

I have to go.
Трябва да тръгвам.
[trʲábva da trégvam]

I will be right back.
Сега ще се върна.
[segá ʃte se vérna]

It's late.
Вече е късно.
[vétʃe e kásno]

I have to get up early.
Трябва рано да ставам.
[trʲábva ráno da stávam]

I'm leaving tomorrow.
Аз заминавам утре.
[az zaminávam útre]

We're leaving tomorrow.
Ние утре заминаваме.
[nie útre zaminávame]

Have a nice trip!
Щастливо пътуване!
[ʃtastlívo pətúvane!]

It was nice meeting you.
Беше ми приятно да се запознаем.
[béʃe mi prijátno da se zapoznáem]

It was nice talking to you.
Беше ми приятно да поговоря с вас.
[béʃe mi prijátno da pogovórʲa s vas]

Thanks for everything.
Благодаря за всичко.
[blagodarʲá za fsítʃko]

I had a very good time.

Прекрасно прекарах времето.
[prekrásno prekárah vrémeto]

We had a very good time.

Ние прекрасно прекарахме времето.
[nie prekrásno prekárahme vrémeto]

It was really great.

Всичкото беше страхотно.
[fsítʃkoto béʃe strahótno]

I'm going to miss you.

Ще скучая.
[ʃte skutʃája]

We're going to miss you.

Ние ще скучаем.
[nie ʃte skutʃáem]

Good luck!

Късмет! Успех!
[kəsmét! uspéh!]

Say hi to …

Предайте поздрави на …
[predájte pózdravi na …]

Foreign language

I don't understand.	**Аз не разбирам.** [az ne razbíram]
Write it down, please.	**Напишете това, моля.** [napíʃéte tová, mólʲa]
Do you speak ...?	**Знаете ли ...?** [znáete li ...?]
I speak a little bit of ...	**Малко знам ...** [málko znam ...]
English	**английски** [anglíjski]
Turkish	**турски** [túrski]
Arabic	**арабски** [arápski]
French	**френски** [frénski]
German	**немски** [némski]
Italian	**италиански** [italiánski]
Spanish	**испански** [ispánski]
Portuguese	**португалски** [portugálski]
Chinese	**китайски** [kitájski]
Japanese	**японски** [japónski]
Can you repeat that, please.	**Повторете, моля.** [poftoréte, mólʲa]
I understand.	**Аз разбирам.** [az razbíram]
I don't understand.	**Аз не разбирам.** [az ne razbíram]
Please speak more slowly.	**Говорете по-бавно, моля.** [govórete po-bávno, mólʲa]
Is that correct? (Am I saying it right?)	**Това правилно ли е?** [tová právilno li e?]
What is this? (What does this mean?)	**Какво е това?** [kakvó e tová?]

Apologies

Excuse me, please.
Извинете, моля.
[izvinéte, mólʲa]

I'm sorry.
Съжалявам.
[səʒalʲávam]

I'm really sorry.
Много съжалявам.
[mnógo səʒalʲávam]

Sorry, it's my fault.
Виновен съм, вината е моя.
[vinóven səm, vináta e mója]

My mistake.
Грешката е моя.
[greʃkata e mója]

May I ...?
Мога ли ...?
[móga li ...?]

Do you mind if I ...?
Имате ли нещо против, ако аз ...?
[ímate li néʃto protív, akó az ...?]

It's OK.
Няма нищо.
[nʲáma níʃto]

It's all right.
Всичко е наред.
[fsíʧko e naréd]

Don't worry about it.
Не се безпокойте.
[ne se bespokójte]

Agreement

Yes. **Да.**
[da]

Yes, sure. **Да, разбира се.**
[da, razbíra se]

OK (Good!) **Добре!**
[dobré!]

Very well. **Много добре!**
[mnógo dobré!]

Certainly! **Разбира се!**
[razbíra se!]

I agree. **Съгласен /съгласна/ съм.**
[səglásen /səglásna/ səm]

That's correct. **Вярно.**
[vʲárno]

That's right. **Правилно.**
[právilno]

You're right. **Прав /права/ сте.**
[prav /práva/ ste]

I don't mind. **Не възразявам.**
[ne vəzrazʲávam]

Absolutely right. **Абсолютно вярно.**
[absolʲútno vʲárno]

It's possible. **Това е възможно.**
[tová e vəzmóʒno]

That's a good idea. **Това е добра идея.**
[tová e dobrá idéja]

I can't say no. **Не мога да откажа.**
[ne móga da otкáʒa]

I'd be happy to. **Ще се радвам.**
[ʃte se rádvam]

With pleasure. **С удоволствие.**
[s udovólstvie]

Refusal. Expressing doubt

No.
Не.
[ne]

Certainly not.
Не, разбира се.
[ne, razbíra se]

I don't agree.
Аз не съм съгласен /съгласна/.
[az ne səm səglásen /səglásna/]

I don't think so.
Аз не мисля така.
[az ne míslʲa taká]

It's not true.
Това не е вярно.
[tová ne e vʲárno]

You are wrong.
Грешите.
[greʃíte]

I think you are wrong.
Мисля, че грешите.
[míslʲa, tʃe greʃíte]

I'm not sure.
Не съм сигурен /сигурна/.
[ne səm síguren /sígurna/]

It's impossible.
Това не е възможно.
[tová ne e vəzmóʒno]

Nothing of the kind (sort)!
Нищо подобно!
[níʃto podóbno!]

The exact opposite.
Напротив!
[naprótiv!]

I'm against it.
Аз съм против.
[az səm protív]

I don't care.
На мен ми е все едно.
[na men mi e fse ednó]

I have no idea.
Нямам представа.
[nʲámam pretstáva]

I doubt it.
Съмнявам се, че е така.
[səmnʲávam se, tʃe e taká]

Sorry, I can't.
Извинете ме, аз не мога.
[izvinéte me, az ne móga]

Sorry, I don't want to.
Извинете ме, аз не искам.
[izvinéte me, az ne ískam]

Thank you, but I don't need this.
Благодаря, това не ми трябва.
[blagodarʲá, tová ne mi trʲábva]

It's getting late.
Вече е късно.
[vétʃe e kə́sno]

I have to get up early.

Трябва рано да ставам.
[tri̯ábva ráno da stávam]

I don't feel well.

Чувствам се зле.
[t͡ʃúfstvam se zle]

Expressing gratitude

Thank you.	**Благодаря.** [blagodar'á]
Thank you very much.	**Много благодаря.** [mnógo blagodar'á]
I really appreciate it.	**Много съм признателен** **/признателна/.** [mnógo səm priznátelen /priznátelna/]
I'm really grateful to you.	**Много съм ви благодарен** **/благодарна/.** [mnógo səm vi blagodáren /blagodárna/]
We are really grateful to you.	**Ние сме ви благодарни.** [nie sme vi blagodárni]
Thank you for your time.	**Благодаря ви, че отделихте време.** [blagodar'á vi, ʧe otdelíhte vréme]
Thanks for everything.	**Благодаря за всичко.** [blagodar'á za fsíʧko]
Thank you for …	**Благодаря за …** [blagodar'á za …]
your help	**вашата помощ** [váʃata pómoʃt]
a nice time	**хубавото време** [húbavoto vréme]
a wonderful meal	**чудната храна** [ʧúdnata hraná]
a pleasant evening	**приятната вечер** [prijátnata véʧer]
a wonderful day	**прекрасния ден** [prekrásnija den]
an amazing journey	**интересната екскурзия** [interésnata ekskúrzija]
Don't mention it.	**Няма за що.** [n'áma za ʃto]
You are welcome.	**Моля.** [mól'a]
Any time.	**Винаги моля.** [vínagi mól'a]
My pleasure.	**Радвам се, че помогнах.** [rádvam se, ʧe pomógnah]

Forget it.

Забравете.
[zabravéte]

Don't worry about it.

Не се безпокойте.
[ne se bespokójte]

Congratulations. Best wishes

Congratulations!	**Поздравявам!** [pozdravʲávam!]
Happy birthday!	**Честит рожден ден!** [ʧestít roʒdén den!]
Merry Christmas!	**Весела Коледа!** [vésela kóleda!]
Happy New Year!	**Честита Нова година!** [ʧestíta nóva godína!]
Happy Easter!	**Честит Великден!** [ʧestít velíkden!]
Happy Hanukkah!	**Честита Ханука!** [ʧestíta hánuka!]
I'd like to propose a toast.	**Имам тост.** [ímam tost]
Cheers!	**За вашето здраве!** [za váʃeto zdráve!]
Let's drink to …!	**Да пием за …!** [da piém za …!]
To our success!	**За нашия успех!** [za náʃija uspéh!]
To your success!	**За вашия успех!** [za váʃija uspéh!]
Good luck!	**Късмет!** [kəsmét!]
Have a nice day!	**Приятен ден!** [prijáten den!]
Have a good holiday!	**Хубава почивка!** [húbava poʧífka!]
Have a safe journey!	**Успешно пътуване!** [uspéʃno pətúvane!]
I hope you get better soon!	**Желая ви скорошно оздравяване!** [ʒelája vi skóroʃno ozdravʲávane!]

Socializing

Why are you sad?	**Защо сте разстроени?** [zaʃtó ste rasstróeni?]
Smile! Cheer up!	**Усмихнете се!** [usmihnéte se!]
Are you free tonight?	**Заети ли сте днес вечерта?** [zaéti li ste dnes vetʃertá?]

May I offer you a drink?	**Мога ли да ви предложа едно питие?** [móga li da vi predlóʒa ednó pitié?]
Would you like to dance?	**Искате ли да танцувате?** [ískate li da tantsúvate?]
Let's go to the movies.	**Да отидем ли на кино?** [da otídem li na kíno?]

May I invite you to ...?	**Мога ли да ви поканя на ...?** [móga li da vi pokánʲa na ...?]
a restaurant	**ресторант** [restoránt]
the movies	**кино** [kíno]
the theater	**театър** [teátər]
go for a walk	**на разходка** [na rashótka]

At what time?	**В колко?** [v kólko?]
tonight	**днес вечерта** [dnes vetʃertá]
at six	**в 6 часа** [v ʃest tʃasá]
at seven	**в 7 часа** [v sédem tʃasá]
at eight	**в 8 часа** [v ósem tʃasá]
at nine	**в 9 часа** [v dévet tʃasá]

Do you like it here?	**Харесва ли ви тук?** [harésva li vi tuk?]
Are you here with someone?	**С някой ли сте тук?** [s nʲákoj li ste tuk?]

I'm with my friend.	**Аз съм с приятел /приятелка/.** [az səm s prijátel /prijátelka/]
I'm with my friends.	**Аз съм с приятели.** [az səm s prijáteli]
No, I'm alone.	**Аз съм сам /сама/.** [az səm sam /samá/]
Do you have a boyfriend?	**Имаш ли приятел?** [ímaʃ li prijátel?]
I have a boyfriend.	**Аз имам приятел.** [az ímam prijátel]
Do you have a girlfriend?	**Имаш ли приятелка?** [ímaʃ li prijátelka?]
I have a girlfriend.	**Аз имам гадже.** [az ímam gádʒe]
Can I see you again?	**Ще се видим ли още?** [ʃte se vídim li oʃté?]
Can I call you?	**Мога ли да ти се обадя?** [móga li da ti se obádʲa?]
Call me. (Give me a call.)	**Обади ми се.** [obádi mi se]
What's your number?	**Какъв ти е номерът?** [kakév ti e nómerət?]
I miss you.	**Липсваш ми.** [lípsvaʃ mi]
You have a beautiful name.	**Имате много красиво име.** [ímate mnógo krasívo íme]
I love you.	**Аз те обичам.** [az te obítʃam]
Will you marry me?	**Омъжи се за мен.** [oméʒi se za men]
You're kidding!	**Шегувате се!** [ʃegúvate se!]
I'm just kidding.	**Аз само се шегувам.** [az sámo se ʃegúvam]
Are you serious?	**Сериозно ли говорите?** [serózno li govórite?]
I'm serious.	**Сериозен /сериозна/ съм.** [serózen /serózna/ səm]
Really?!	**Наистина ли?!** [naístina li?!]
It's unbelievable!	**Това е невероятно!** [tová e neverojátno!]
I don't believe you.	**Не ви вярвам.** [ne vi vʲárvam]
I can't.	**Аз не мога.** [az ne móga]
I don't know.	**Аз не знам.** [az ne znam]

I don't understand you.   **Аз не ви разбирам.**
[az ne vi razbíram]

Please go away.   **Вървете си, моля.**
[vərvéte si, mól'a]

Leave me alone!   **Оставете ме на мира!**
[ostávete me na mirá!]

I can't stand him.   **Не го понасям.**
[ne go ponás'am]

You are disgusting!   **Отвратителен сте!**
[otvratítelen ste!]

I'll call the police!   **Ще повикам полиция!**
[ʃte póvikam polítsija!]

Sharing impressions. Emotions

I like it.	**Това ми харесва.** [tová mi harésva]
Very nice.	**Много мило.** [mnógo mílo]
That's great!	**Това е страхотно!** [tová e strahótno!]
It's not bad.	**Не е лошо.** [ne e lóʃo]
I don't like it.	**Това не ми харесва.** [tová ne mi harésva]
It's not good.	**Това не е добре.** [tová ne e dobré]
It's bad.	**Това е лошо.** [tová e lóʃo]
It's very bad.	**Това е много лошо.** [tová e mnógo lóʃo]
It's disgusting.	**Това е отвратително.** [tová e otvratítelno]
I'm happy.	**Щастлив /щастлива/ съм.** [ʃtastlív /ʃtastlíva/ səm]
I'm content.	**Доволен /доволна/ съм.** [dovólen /dovólna/ səm]
I'm in love.	**Влюбен /влюбена/ съм.** [vlʲúben /vlʲúbena/ səm]
I'm calm.	**Спокоен /спокойна/ съм.** [spokóen /spokójna/ səm]
I'm bored.	**Скучно ми е.** [skútʃno mi e]
I'm tired.	**Аз се изморих.** [az se izmoríh]
I'm sad.	**Тъжно ми е.** [téʒno mi e]
I'm frightened.	**Уплашен /уплашена/ съм.** [upláʃen /upláʃena/ səm]
I'm angry.	**Ядосвам се.** [jadósvam se]
I'm worried.	**Вълнувам се.** [vəlnúvam se]
I'm nervous.	**Аз нервнича.** [az nérvnitʃa]

I'm jealous. (envious)

Аз завиждам.
[az zavíʒdam]

I'm surprised.

Учуден /учудена/ съм.
[utʃúden /utʃúdena/ səm]

I'm perplexed.

Аз съм объркан /объркана/.
[az səm obérkan /obérkana/]

Problems. Accidents

I've got a problem.	**Аз имам проблем.** [az ímam problém]
We've got a problem.	**Ние имаме проблем.** [nie ímame problém]
I'm lost.	**Аз се заблудих.** [az se zablúdih]
I missed the last bus (train).	**Аз закъснях за последния автобус (влак).** [az zakəsnʲáh za poslédniʲa aftobús (vlak)]
I don't have any money left.	**Не ми останаха никакви пари.** [ne mi ostánaha níkakvi parí]

I've lost my ...	**Аз загубих ...** [az zagúbih ...]
Someone stole my ...	**Откраднаха ми ...** [otkrádnaha mi ...]
passport	**паспорта** [paspórta]
wallet	**портмонето** [portmonéto]
papers	**документите** [dokuméntite]
ticket	**билета** [biléta]

money	**парите** [paríte]
handbag	**чантата** [tʃántata]
camera	**фотоапарата** [fotoaparáta]
laptop	**лаптопа** [laptópa]
tablet computer	**таблета** [tabléta]
mobile phone	**телефона** [telefóna]

Help me!	**Помогнете!** [pomognéte!]
What's happened?	**Какво се случи?** [kakvó se slutʃí?]

fire	**пожар** [poʒár]
shooting	**стрелба** [strelbá]
murder	**убийство** [ubíjstvo]
explosion	**взрив** [vzriv]
fight	**бой** [boj]

Call the police!	**Извикайте полиция!** [izvikájte polítsija!]
Please hurry up!	**Моля, по-бързо!** [mólʲa, po-bérzo!]
I'm looking for the police station.	**Аз търся полицейски участък.** [az térsʲa politséjski uʹʧastək]
I need to make a call.	**Трябва да се обадя.** [trʲábva da se obádʲa]
May I use your phone?	**Мога ли да се обадя?** [móga li da se obádʲa?]

I've been …	**Мен ме …** [men me …]
mugged	**ограбиха** [ográbiha]
robbed	**обраха** [obráha]
raped	**изнасилиха** [iznasíliha]
attacked (beaten up)	**пребиха** [prebíha]

Are you all right?	**Всичко ли е наред?** [fsíʧko li e naréd?]
Did you see who it was?	**Видяхте ли, кой беше?** [vidʲáhte li, koj béʃe?]
Would you be able to recognize the person?	**Ще можете ли да го познаете?** [ʃte móʒete li da go poznáete?]
Are you sure?	**Сигурен /сигурна/ ли сте?** [síguren /sígurna/ li ste?]

Please calm down.	**Моля, да се успокоите.** [mólʲa, da se uspokóite]
Take it easy!	**По-спокойно!** [po-spokójno!]
Don't worry!	**Не се безпокойте.** [ne se bespokójte]
Everything will be fine.	**Всичко ще се оправи.** [fsíʧko ʃte se oprávi]
Everything's all right.	**Всичко е наред.** [fsíʧko e naréd]

Come here, please.

Елате, моля.
[eláte, mólʲa]

I have some questions for you.

Имам няколко въпроса към Вас.
[ímam nʲakólko vəprósa kəm vas]

Wait a moment, please.

Изчакайте, моля.
[iztʃákajte, mólʲa]

Do you have any I.D.?

Имате ли документи?
[ímate li dokuménti?]

Thanks. You can leave now.

Благодаря. Свободни сте.
[blagodarʲá. svobódni ste]

Hands behind your head!

Ръцете зад тила!
[rətséte zat tíla!]

You're under arrest!

Арестуван /арестувана/ сте!
[arestúvan /arestúvana/ ste!]

Health problems

Please help me.
Помогнете, моля.
[pomognéte, mólʲa]

I don't feel well.
Лошо ми е.
[lóʃo mi e]

My husband doesn't feel well.
На мъжа ми му е лошо.
[na məʒá mi mu e lóʃo]

My son ...
На сина ми ...
[na siná mi ...]

My father ...
На баща ми ...
[na baʃtá mi ...]

My wife doesn't feel well.
На жена ми и е лошо.
[na ʒená mi i e lóʃo]

My daughter ...
На дъщеря ми ...
[na dəʃterʲá mi ...]

My mother ...
На майка ми ...
[na májka mi ...]

I've got a ...
Боли ме ...
[bolí me ...]

headache
главата
[glaváta]

sore throat
гърлото
[gérloto]

stomach ache
корема
[koréma]

toothache
зъба
[zéba]

I feel dizzy.
Ви е ми се свят.
[vi e mi se svʲat]

He has a fever.
Той има температура.
[toj íma temperatúra]

She has a fever.
Тя има температура.
[tʲa íma temperatúra]

I can't breathe.
Аз не мога да дишам.
[az ne móga da díʃam]

I'm short of breath.
Аз се задъхвам.
[az se zadéhvam]

I am asthmatic.
Аз съм астматик.
[az səm astmatík]

I am diabetic.
Аз съм диабетик.
[az səm diabetík]

I can't sleep.	**Имам безсъние.**
	[ímam bessénie]
food poisoning	**хранително отравяне**
	[hranítelno otrávʲane]

It hurts here.	**Тук ме боли.**
	[tuk me bolí]
Help me!	**Помогнете!**
	[pomognéte!]
I am here!	**Аз съм тук!**
	[az səm tuk!]
We are here!	**Ние сме тук!**
	[nie sme tuk!]
Get me out of here!	**Извадете ме!**
	[izvadéte me!]
I need a doctor.	**Трябва ми лекар.**
	[trʲábva mi lékar]
I can't move.	**Не мога да мърдам.**
	[ne móga da mérdam]
I can't move my legs.	**Не си чувствам краката.**
	[ne si ʧúfstvam krakáta]

I have a wound.	**Аз съм ранен /ранена/.**
	[az səm ránen /ránena/]
Is it serious?	**Сериозно ли е?**
	[seriózno li e?]
My documents are in my pocket.	**Документите ми са в джоба.**
	[dokuméntite mi sa v dʒóba]
Calm down!	**Успокойте се!**
	[uspokójte se!]
May I use your phone?	**Мога ли да се обадя?**
	[móga li da se obádʲa?]

Call an ambulance!	**Повикайте бърза помощ!**
	[povikájte bérza pómoʃt!]
It's urgent!	**Това е спешно!**
	[tová e spéʃno!]
It's an emergency!	**Това е много спешно!**
	[tová e mnógo spéʃno!]
Please hurry up!	**Моля, по-бързо!**
	[mólʲa, po-bérzo!]
Would you please call a doctor?	**Повикайте лекар, моля.**
	[povikájte lékar, mólʲa]
Where is the hospital?	**Кажете, моля, къде е болницата?**
	[kaʒéte, mólʲa, kədé e bólnitsata?]

How are you feeling?	**Как се чувствате?**
	[kak se ʧúfstvate]
Are you all right?	**Всичко ли е наред?**
	[fsíʧko li e naréd?]
What's happened?	**Какво се случи?**
	[kakvó se sluʧí?]

I feel better now.

Вече ми е по-добре.
[vétʃe mi e po-dobré]

It's OK.

Всичко е наред.
[fsítʃko e naréd]

It's all right.

Всичко е наред.
[fsítʃko e naréd]

At the pharmacy

pharmacy (drugstore)	**аптека** [aptéka]
24-hour pharmacy	**денонощна аптека** [denonóʃtna aptéka]
Where is the closest pharmacy?	**Къде е най-близката аптека?** [kədé e naj-blízkata aptéka?]
Is it open now?	**Сега отворена ли е?** [segá otvórena li e?]
At what time does it open?	**В колко се отваря?** [v kólko se otvárʲa?]
At what time does it close?	**До колко работи?** [do kólko ráboti?]
Is it far?	**Далече ли е?** [dalétʃe li e?]
Can I get there on foot?	**Ще стигна ли дотам пеша?** [ʃte stígna li dotám péʃa?]
Can you show me on the map?	**Покажете ми на картата, моля.** [pokaʒéte mi na kártata, mólʲa]
Please give me something for ...	**Дайте ми нещо за ...** [dájte mi néʃto za ...]
a headache	**главоболие** [glavobólie]
a cough	**кашлица** [káʃlitsa]
a cold	**настинка** [nastínka]
the flu	**грип** [grip]
a fever	**температура** [temperatúra]
a stomach ache	**болки в стомаха** [bólki v stomáha]
nausea	**повръщане** [povréʃtane]
diarrhea	**диария** [diárija]
constipation	**запек** [zápek]
pain in the back	**болки в гърба** [bólki v gérba]

chest pain	**болки в гърдите** [bólki v gərdíte]
side stitch	**болки отстрани** [bólki otstraní]
abdominal pain	**болки в корема** [bólki v koréma]

pill	**таблетка** [tablétka]
ointment, cream	**маз, мехлем, крем** [maz, mehlém, krem]
syrup	**сироп** [siróp]
spray	**спрей** [sprej]
drops	**капки** [kápki]

You need to go to the hospital.	**Трябва да отидете в болница.** [triábva da otidéte v bólnitsa]
health insurance	**застраховка** [zastrahófka]
prescription	**рецепта** [retsépta]
insect repellant	**препарат от насекоми** [preparát ot nasekómi]
Band Aid	**лейкопласт** [lejkoplást]

The bare minimum

Excuse me, ...	**Извинете, ...** [izvinéte, ...]
Hello.	**Здравейте.** [zdravéjte]
Thank you.	**Благодаря.** [blagodar'á]
Good bye.	**Довиждане.** [dovíʒdane]
Yes.	**Да.** [da]
No.	**Не.** [ne]
I don't know.	**Аз не знам.** [az ne znam]
Where?	Where to?	When?	**Къде?	Накъде?	Кога?** [kədé?	nakədé?	kogá?]

I need ...	**Трябва ми ...** [tr'ábva mi ...]
I want ...	**Аз искам ...** [az ískam ...]
Do you have ...?	**Имате ли ...?** [ímate li ...?]
Is there a ... here?	**Тук има ли ...?** [tuk íma li ...?]
May I ...?	**Мога ли ...?** [móga li ...?]
..., please (polite request)	**Моля.** [mól'a]

I'm looking for ...	**Аз търся ...** [az tɨrs'a ...]
the restroom	**тоалетна** [toalétna]
an ATM	**банкомат** [bankomát]
a pharmacy (drugstore)	**аптека** [aptéka]
a hospital	**болница** [bólnitsa]
the police station	**полицейски участък** [politséjski utʃástək]
the subway	**метро** [metró]

a taxi	такси
	[táksi]
the train station	гара
	[gára]

My name is ...	Казвам се ...
	[kázvam se ...]
What's your name?	Как се казвате?
	[kak se kázvate?]
Could you please help me?	Помогнете ми, моля.
	[pomognéte mi, mólʲa]
I've got a problem.	Аз имам проблем.
	[az ímam problém]
I don't feel well.	Лошо ми е.
	[lóʃo mi e]
Call an ambulance!	Повикайте бърза помощ!
	[povikájte bérza pómoʃt!]
May I make a call?	Може ли да се обадя?
	[móʒe li da se obádʲa?]

I'm sorry.	Извинявам се.
	[izvinʲávam se]
You're welcome.	Моля.
	[mólʲa]

I, me	аз
	[az]
you (inform.)	ти
	[ti]
he	той
	[toj]
she	тя
	[tʲa]
they (masc.)	те
	[te]
they (fem.)	те
	[te]
we	ние
	[nie]
you (pl)	вие
	[víe]
you (sg, form.)	Вие
	[víe]

ENTRANCE	ВХОД
	[vhod]
EXIT	ИЗХОД
	[íshot]
OUT OF ORDER	НЕ РАБОТИ
	[ne ráboti]
CLOSED	ЗАТВОРЕНО
	[zatvóreno]

OPEN

ОТВОРЕНО
[otvóreno]

FOR WOMEN

ЗА ЖЕНИ
[za ʒení]

FOR MEN

ЗА МЪЖЕ
[za məʒé]

MINI DICTIONARY

This section contains 250
useful words required for
everyday communication.
You will find the names of
months and days of the week
here. The dictionary also
contains topics such as colors,
measurements, family, and
more

T&P Books Publishing

DICTIONARY CONTENTS

T&P Books Publishing

time	**време** (с)	[vréme]
hour	**час** (м)	[tʃas]
half an hour	**половин час** (м)	[polovín tʃas]
minute	**минута** (ж)	[minúta]
second	**секунда** (ж)	[sekúnda]
today (adv)	**днес**	[dnes]
tomorrow (adv)	**утре**	[útre]
yesterday (adv)	**вчера**	[vtʃéra]
Monday	**понеделник** (м)	[ponedélnik]
Tuesday	**вторник** (м)	[ftórnik]
Wednesday	**сряда** (ж)	[srʲáda]
Thursday	**четвъртък** (м)	[tʃetvértek]
Friday	**петък** (м)	[pétək]
Saturday	**събота** (ж)	[sébota]
Sunday	**неделя** (ж)	[nedélʲa]
day	**ден** (м)	[den]
working day	**работен ден** (м)	[rabóten den]
public holiday	**празничен ден** (м)	[práznitʃen den]
weekend	**почивни дни** (м мн)	[potʃívni dni]
week	**седмица** (ж)	[sédmitsa]
last week (adv)	**през миналата седмица**	[pres mínalata sédmitsa]
next week (adv)	**през следващата седмица**	[pres slédvaʃtata sédmitsa]
in the morning	**сутринта**	[sutrintá]
in the afternoon	**следобед**	[sledóbet]
in the evening	**вечер**	[vétʃer]
tonight (this evening)	**довечера**	[dovétʃera]
at night	**нощем**	[nóʃtem]
midnight	**полунощ** (ж)	[polunóʃt]
January	**януари** (м)	[januári]
February	**февруари** (м)	[fevruári]
March	**март** (м)	[mart]
April	**април** (м)	[apríl]
May	**май** (м)	[maj]
June	**юни** (м)	[júni]
July	**юли** (м)	[júli]
August	**август** (м)	[ávgust]

September	септември (м)	[septémvri]
October	октомври (м)	[októmvri]
November	ноември (м)	[noémvri]
December	декември (м)	[dekémvri]

in spring	през пролетта	[prez prolettá]
in summer	през лятото	[prez ľátoto]
in fall	през есента	[prez esentá]
in winter	през зимата	[prez zímata]

month	месец (м)	[mésets]
season (summer, etc.)	сезон (м)	[sezón]
year	година (ж)	[godína]

2. Numbers. Numerals

0 zero	нула (ж)	[núla]
1 one	едно	[ednó]
2 two	две	[dve]
3 three	три	[tri]
4 four	четири	[ʧétiri]

5 five	пет	[pet]
6 six	шест	[ʃest]
7 seven	седем	[sédem]
8 eight	осем	[ósem]
9 nine	девет	[dévet]
10 ten	десет	[déset]

11 eleven	единадесет	[edinádeset]
12 twelve	дванадесет	[dvanádeset]
13 thirteen	тринадесет	[trinádeset]
14 fourteen	четиринадесет	[ʧetirinádeset]
15 fifteen	петнадесет	[petnádeset]

16 sixteen	шестнадесет	[ʃesnádeset]
17 seventeen	седемнадесет	[sedemnádeset]
18 eighteen	осемнадесет	[osemnádeset]
19 nineteen	деветнадесет	[devetnádeset]

20 twenty	двадесет	[dvádeset]
30 thirty	тридесет	[trídeset]
40 forty	четиридесет	[ʧetírideset]
50 fifty	петдесет	[petdesét]

60 sixty	шестдесет	[ʃestdesét]
70 seventy	седемдесет	[sedemdesét]
80 eighty	осемдесет	[osemdesét]
90 ninety	деветдесет	[devetdesét]
100 one hundred	сто	[sto]

200 two hundred	двеста	[dvésta]
300 three hundred	триста	[trísta]
400 four hundred	четиристотин	[tʃétiri·stótin]
500 five hundred	петстотин	[pét·stótin]
600 six hundred	шестстотин	[ʃést·stótin]
700 seven hundred	седемстотин	[sédem·stótin]
800 eight hundred	осемстотин	[ósem·stótin]
900 nine hundred	деветстотин	[dévet·stótin]
1000 one thousand	хиляда (ж)	[hilʲáda]
10000 ten thousand	десет хиляди	[déset hílʲadi]
one hundred thousand	сто хиляди	[sto hílʲadi]
million	милион (м)	[milión]
billion	милиард (м)	[miliárt]

3. Humans. Family

man (adult male)	мъж (м)	[məʒ]
young man	младеж (м)	[mladéʒ]
woman	жена (ж)	[ʒená]
girl (young woman)	девойка (ж)	[devójka]
old man	старец (м)	[stárets]
old woman	старица (ж)	[stáritsa]
mother	майка (ж)	[májka]
father	баща (м)	[baʃtá]
son	син (м)	[sin]
daughter	дъщеря (ж)	[dəʃterʲá]
brother	брат (м)	[brat]
sister	сестра (ж)	[sestrá]
parents	родители (м мн)	[rodíteli]
child	дете (с)	[deté]
children	деца (с мн)	[detsá]
stepmother	мащеха (ж)	[máʃteha]
stepfather	пасток (м)	[pástrok]
grandmother	баба (ж)	[bába]
grandfather	дядо (м)	[dʲádo]
grandson	внук (м)	[vnuk]
granddaughter	внучка (ж)	[vnútʃka]
grandchildren	внуци (м мн)	[vnútsi]
uncle	вуйчо (м)	[vújtʃo]
aunt	леля (ж)	[lélʲa]
nephew	племенник (м)	[plémennik]
niece	племенница (ж)	[plémennitsa]
wife	жена (ж)	[ʒená]

husband	мъж (м)	[məʒ]
married (masc.)	женен	[ʒénen]
married (fem.)	омъжена	[oméʒena]
widow	вдовица (ж)	[vdovítsa]
widower	вдовец (м)	[vdovéts]

| name (first name) | име (с) | [íme] |
| surname (last name) | фамилия (ж) | [famílija] |

relative	роднина (м, ж)	[rodnína]
friend (masc.)	приятел (м)	[prijátel]
friendship	приятелство (с)	[prijátelstvo]

partner	партньор (м)	[partnʲór]
superior (n)	началник (м)	[natʃálnik]
colleague	колега (м, ж)	[koléga]
neighbors	съседи (м мн)	[səsédi]

4. Human body

body	тяло (с)	[tʲálo]
heart	сърце (с)	[sərtsé]
blood	кръв (ж)	[krəv]
brain	мозък (м)	[mózək]

bone	кост (ж)	[kost]
spine (backbone)	гръбнак (м)	[grəbnák]
rib	ребро (с)	[rebró]
lungs	бели дробове (м мн)	[béli dróbove]
skin	кожа (ж)	[kóʒa]

head	глава (ж)	[glavá]
face	лице (с)	[litsé]
nose	нос (м)	[nos]
forehead	чело (с)	[tʃeló]
cheek	буза (ж)	[búza]

mouth	уста (ж)	[ustá]
tongue	език (м)	[ezík]
tooth	зъб (м)	[zəp]
lips	устни (ж мн)	[ústni]
chin	брадичка (ж)	[bradítʃka]

ear	ухо (с)	[uhó]
neck	шия (ж)	[ʃíja]
eye	око (с)	[okó]
pupil	зеница (ж)	[zénitsa]
eyebrow	вежда (ж)	[véʒda]
eyelash	мигла (ж)	[mígla]
hair	коса (ж)	[kosá]

hairstyle	прическа (ж)	[pritʃéska]
mustache	мустаци (м мн)	[mustátsi]
beard	брада (ж)	[bradá]
to have (a beard, etc.)	нося	[nósʲa]
bald (adj)	плешив	[pleʃív]

hand	китка (ж)	[kítka]
arm	ръка (ж)	[rəká]
finger	пръст (м)	[prəst]
nail	нокът (м)	[nókət]
palm	длан (ж)	[dlan]

shoulder	рамо (с)	[rámo]
leg	крак (м)	[krak]
knee	коляно (с)	[kolʲáno]
heel	пета (ж)	[petá]
back	гръб (м)	[grəp]

5. Clothing. Personal accessories

clothes	облекло (с)	[oblekló]
coat (overcoat)	палто (с)	[paltó]
fur coat	кожено палто (с)	[kóʒeno paltó]
jacket (e.g., leather ~)	яке (с)	[jáke]
raincoat (trenchcoat, etc.)	шлифер (м)	[ʃlífer]

shirt (button shirt)	риза (ж)	[ríza]
pants	панталон (м)	[pantalón]
suit jacket	сако (с)	[sakó]
suit	костюм (м)	[kostʲúm]

dress (frock)	рокля (ж)	[róklʲa]
skirt	пола (ж)	[polá]
T-shirt	терниска (ж)	[téniska]
bathrobe	хавлиен халат (м)	[havlíen halát]
pajamas	пижама (ж)	[piʒáma]
workwear	работно облекло (с)	[rabótno oblekló]

underwear	бельо (с)	[belʲó]
socks	чорапи (м мн)	[tʃorápi]
bra	сутиен (м)	[sutién]
pantyhose	чорапогащник (м)	[tʃorapogáʃtnik]
stockings (thigh highs)	чорапи (м мн)	[tʃorápi]
bathing suit	бански костюм (м)	[bánski kostʲúm]

hat	шапка (ж)	[ʃápka]
footwear	обувки (ж мн)	[obúfki]
boots (e.g., cowboy ~)	ботуши (м мн)	[botúʃi]
heel	ток (м)	[tok]
shoestring	връзка (ж)	[vréska]

shoe polish	крем (м) за обувки	[krem za obúfki]
gloves	ръкавици (ж мн)	[rəkavítsi]
mittens	ръкавици (ж мн) с един пърст	[rəkavítsi s edín pərst]

scarf (muffler)	шал (м)	[ʃal]
glasses (eyeglasses)	очила (мн)	[otʃilá]
umbrella	чадър (м)	[tʃadér]

tie (necktie)	вратовръзка (ж)	[vratovrézka]
handkerchief	носна кърпичка (ж)	[nósna kérpitʃka]
comb	гребен (м)	[grében]
hairbrush	четка (ж) за коса	[tʃétka za kosá]

buckle	катарама (ж)	[kataráma]
belt	колан (м)	[kolán]
purse	чантичка (ж)	[tʃántitʃka]

6. House. Apartment

apartment	апартамент (м)	[apartamént]
room	стая (ж)	[stája]
bedroom	спалня (ж)	[spáln'a]
dining room	столова (ж)	[stolová]

living room	гостна (ж)	[góstna]
study (home office)	кабинет (м)	[kabinét]
entry room	антре (с)	[antré]
bathroom (room with a bath or shower)	баня (ж)	[bán'a]
half bath	тоалетна (ж)	[toalétna]

vacuum cleaner	прахосмукачка (ж)	[praho·smukátʃka]
mop	четка (ж) за под	[tʃétka za pot]
dust cloth	парцал (м)	[partsál]
short broom	метла (ж)	[metlá]
dustpan	лопатка (ж) за боклук	[lopátka za boklúk]

furniture	мебели (мн)	[mébeli]
table	маса (ж)	[mása]
chair	стол (м)	[stol]
armchair	фотьойл (м)	[fot'ójl]

mirror	огледало (с)	[ogledálo]
carpet	килим (м)	[kilím]
fireplace	камина (ж)	[kamína]
drapes	пердета (с мн)	[perdéta]
table lamp	лампа (ж) за маса	[lámpa za mása]
chandelier	полилей (м)	[poliléj]
kitchen	кухня (ж)	[kúhn'a]
gas stove (range)	газова печка (ж)	[gázova pétʃka]

| electric stove | електрическа печка (ж) | [elektrítʃeska pétʃka] |
| microwave oven | микровълнова печка (ж) | [mikrovélnova pétʃka] |

refrigerator	хладилник (м)	[hladílnik]
freezer	фризер (м)	[frízer]
dishwasher	съдомиялна машина (ж)	[sədomijálna maʃína]
faucet	смесител (м)	[smesítel]

meat grinder	месомелачка (ж)	[meso·melátʃka]
juicer	сокоизстисквачка (ж)	[soko·isstiskvátʃka]
toaster	тостер (м)	[tóster]
mixer	миксер (м)	[míkser]

coffee machine	кафеварка (ж)	[kafevárka]
kettle	чайник (м)	[tʃájnik]
teapot	чайник (м)	[tʃájnik]

TV set	телевизор (м)	[televízor]
VCR (video recorder)	видео (с)	[vídeo]
iron (e.g., steam ~)	ютия (ж)	[jutíja]
telephone	телефон (м)	[telefón]

www.ingramcontent.com/pod-product-compliance
Lightning Source LLC
Chambersburg PA
CBHW070837050426
42452CB00011B/2322